# Far from
# New York State

# Far from New York State

Matthew Johnson

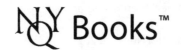

The New York Quarterly Foundation, Inc.
Beacon, New York

NYQ Books™ is an imprint of The New York Quarterly Foundation, Inc.

The New York Quarterly Foundation, Inc.
P. O. Box 470
Beacon, NY 12508

www.nyq.org

First Edition

Set in New Baskerville

Layout and Cover Design by Raymond Hammond

Cover Photo: istock.com/goglik83

Author Photo by Destinee' Allen, Instagram: @d.a.productions

Library of Congress Control Number: 2023931435

ISBN: 978-1-63045-095-3

# Far from New York State

*To my supportive parents, Michael and Wynne,
who have always encouraged me as I found my own
creative passions and outlet. The lives, stories, and
memories you have passed down to me fill the spirit
and margins of these pages.*

# CONTENTS

# Far from New York State

Whoever has made a voyage up the Hudson, must remember
the Kaatskill mountains.

—*Washington Irving,* "Rip Van Winkle"

With God's help I hope to deliver
the message he entrusted to me.

— *Edward Mitchell Bannister*

Nunquam Retrorsum (Never Backward)

— *New Rochelle, New York's Motto*

## On Washington Irving and his Literary Friends
   ## at Sunnyside


They share gossip, Washington Irving and the literary cohort,
Living retorts to the British dig directed at a young, rebel nation:
*Who dares read an American novel?*
In workshop, the minds of the writers churn, like industrial tugboats
   up the Erie Canal.
The Great Experiment of this new republic
Requires validation in literature, and to move the story along,
Like ancient prophets penning the Bible,
So they look to the likes of Irving,
Who sits in the middle of the foreground to provide counsel,
Like an Abraham in a room of Isaacs and Jacobs.
At Sunnyside, the writers craft and talk shop of drafts,
And discuss a multitude of matters and subjects into the early morning,
All while skirting around, like the Founding Fathers who preceded them,
The one thing that casts a shadow upon the Republic,
And the reason, why if I could attend this master class lecture,
My mere presence would very much startle everyone....

# Harriet Peers Down from the Mountaintop

Sister Moses is alone now,
As she was on that first trek through the forests of Maryland and Delaware,
Where the humid nights and fear of capture soaked the air,
And the swamp splashed the sweat and soiled her feet.
Harriet made it to the Promised Land,
Before the flowers of young men were sent down to Dixie to defend
   and die for it.
But then after the Union Army won, its soldiers abandoned
   Southern capitals,
And the Promised Land was pulled under,
As if the New Jerusalem became Hell on Earth.
It's frigid in winter so far upstate,
But not as cold as the way they treat black people now....
The nights are lonely too,
And Harriet hums coded spirituals of yesteryear, to fill the space as company.

# If Only There were Humor in Heaven

Now in Hollywood, Redd Foxx, having long skewed social niceties
    and sacred cows
With a scandalous tongue through countless monologues,
Reminiscences on bouncing around the Chitlin' Circuit
While having his eyes out for sundown towns,
And witnessing the evolution of humor:
From Sweet Poppa Pigmeat to the raw and strutting Murphy.
The soft edges which Fred Sanford put on with a smile,
That same one after zinging a smart-aleck remark at Aunt Esther, is
    no longer an act.
Wrinkles have softened the face, but not the f-words,
Which are still flung like one-liners in his young, nightclub age.
In this Transfiguration of dark comedy on the set of *Harlem Nights,*
God the Father is nicknamed Chicago Red.

# Dark Comedy

*Take it easy.*
*It's just a joke.*
*Lighten up.*

But how could I lighten up,
For there is black on my skin,
And black within my soul?

*Hahaha!*

## Stylish Like Clyde Frazier

In the rebellious, copacetic, folkadelic world
Of late '60s to early'70s New York,
There is no cooler hepcat on the island
Than Clyde, stylin' and profilin' in his Rolls Royce,
Slicin' and dicin' through Manhattan traffic to get back to the penthouse,
And then to The Garden, facilitatin' the offense.

His lapels are dapper. His cashmere suits are sharper.
The gold around his neck and on his wrist is blinding.

Clyde is the grand maestro of basketball in New York,
And with the greatest of dexterity,
Juggles the orange ball of Manhattan in one hand,
And then a night episode with the other.

# A Prescription from Dr. J

First, take enough fish
To save Pittsburgh,
And the floundering ABA
If you can; and also, Philadelphia basketball,
Which had been irrelevant
Since the departure of Wilt Chamberlain.
If lack of playing above the rim persists,
Skywalk to the closest Bill Walton,
And then throw it down
On his curly, red face.

# Jam Sessions at The Garden

Down in the Garden —

Wall Street yuppies assemble
To hobnob and spew curse-word catcalls at Michael Jordan.

Hollywood cool cats strut and pose for cameras,
And then chit chat and trash talk
With Reggie Miller and Larry Bird down in front-row.

Average Joes try to observe the bouncing ball from high in the
    mezzanine level;
It's difficult to read the sights from these heights,
Like trying to sift through scribbled bebop notes of sheet music.

Wonderful basketball, like the one the Knicks used to play,
Can pull you into the finer things of life,

Like shared love of music and art among strangers —

# In Tragedy: Paul Robeson as Othello

The tide of dialogue vocalized in bass baritone
Reverberates through the concert hall,
Reaching to the back of the playhouse
And carrying enough weight to hit late arrivals in the lobby
With the same intensity as the players in the orchestra pit.
Life imitates art for the most Renaissance of men in Paul Robeson,
Boundless as the potential of Othello, and double dying each day:
Once on stage every night from cunning Iago,
And once every minute while stepping foot in America.
So Venice and the United States have their way
And tear down these men of color without mercy.

They took pleasure in chipping away at such genius, black porcelain,
As if itching to knock him down from the mountain of exceptionalism
For even daring to climb in pursuit of liberty and happiness.

# My Uncle's Running Buddy

Before the boy became a man:
*The Man on Fire, The Inside Man,*
Or "The Iceman Cometh,"
Denzel was just another running buddy for my uncle.
They and the neighborhood children
On the south side of Mount Vernon
Marked fire hydrants as endzones,
Played in narrow streets, avoiding parked vehicles,
And sprinted outside as long as summer lasted,
Constantly in pursuit of overthrown Hail Mary passes.
Then as gradual as friendships that drift apart as lives do,
Denzel stayed at that pace right out of Mount Vernon,
As if he were still trying to catch up to dreams,
Like they were deep balls just of reach,
Grazing off the fingertips.

## Prison Meal Dream

The full moon is hung up like butcher shop specials, and I want one.
I would hopscotch atop the stars,
Like I was avoiding construction cones, or a packed sidewalk,
And enter the meat market to get me one of those deals.
I would examine the rib racks and the lamb shanks,
And I would place my arm on the counter,
Drumming on the block to get the attention of the clerk,
And then get something familiar, like steak or hamburgers.
But the moon is not made up of meat or cheese, but rocks,
Like the ones I strum and kick up on the yard....

# Mamma Sings the Prison Blues

The wails of a mother,
Whose child had just been locked away,
Ring out like drunken night gunfire,
And are the kind of sound
That echoes in neighborhood heads for days....

# Mount Vernon Got Game

*For Ray Williams*

Jim Boeheim only has 16 spots on his Orangemen roster.
Then there's lesser so at St. John's, and even fewer at Seton Hall or Iona.
Then there's the limit on scholarship offers,
And then of course, fighting with the one or two walk-ons
Who actually lay out for charges and chase loose balls like bats out of hell.
Urban black boys, crabs in the proverbial barrel,
Play endless games of 21 until they're about to fall apart,
And long after the sunset spun into night.
They bang their chests after shooting and making their high-arching shots,
High enough to douse the full moon.
Their fatigued legs shake like tables in earthquakes, as they play their
    unendable games.
Meekness is tossed aside like sweat-drenched towels in this double-rimmed
    crucible,
For dogged self-confidence is imperative
If someone acts as an obstacle to you becoming the next Ben Gordon....

# Big Apple Blues

Consider me
Like a heartbreak, or a montage,
As you pass by me, and refuse to see me
In the market streets, or on the subway.

I'm new here,
And New York is killing me too;
There's not a soul willing to call my name,
Or to even accidentally stub my toe.

I'll still be here though,
Even if no one notices,
I've just hidden underneath a manhole plate,
And live with the sewer rats.

## Listening to Illmatic

I recite lines into the mirror,
Holding my hairbrush as a microphone,
Mean mugging to an audience of shaving razors and deodorant bars,
And shooting out my fingers like web slingers,
Keeping both emphasis and beat with my hand gestures.

Young black people, jailed, gunned down, or drugged up,
Are reincarnated in rhyme and storytelling,
But it's only in here, in the grooves of music and my makeshift,
   bathroom studio,
And not out there, where the world is not yours,
But is always sadder.

# Red Light District Love

Red Light District Love
Sway your gin-drinkin' hips
And come over here honey,
You ain't about to leave here
Without me whispering
Something nasty in your ear:

*I love you,*

*And I'm here all night*
*For you to smack me hard.*

# Urban Legend of the Bad Samaritans

*For Kitty Genovese*

The lights are on, so somebody must be home:
Giggling stoners pass a semi-glowing joint,
Ponderous children stay up late
To people-watch through bedroom windows,
Partygoers rub up against each other as the music drones,
Lovers thrust and enter one another,
And the restless dreamer tosses and turns,
But nobody heard a word....

# Gin-Soaked Saxophone Solo

I was drinking like a fish,
Trying to blow like Bird,
With my gin-soaked saxophone.

Have you ever drunk
The boogie-woogie brew,
Honey?

I swear I heard the horn was talkin'
After I took a swung from the spirits:
*Use me Daddy-O!* I heard. *Use those lips to hit the right notes...*

I swear the radiator was hissing at me too:
*More fire!* It moaned. *Play more fire!*
The heat was gassing me up to get more down.
My ears began to exhale smoke as I blowed.

I was playing.
I was wailing and running my slippery fingers,
Sloppily, on my saxophone.
I was sweating chords from the back of my throat.

I was playing, then I became lightheaded.
I was losing balance on the edge of my seat.
I fell over....

It was death by music,
And gin and jazz were heaven —

# Apartment Homegoing Service

Not one word was uttered about the deceased,
Or the manner in which they had died.

There were no lamentations or sighs;
There were no screaming, teary-eyed mourners
Shaking their fist to the heavens, as they draped over the coffin,
Pleading to God and grabbing onto the casket, and all attention.

No, the simple ceremony proceeded
As silent as a passing, but unuttered thought.

The celebration of life was attended
By dust mites and overzealous flies, who had no need for prayers
    or burial rites.
There were no sympathy flowers,
But wilting, brown houseplants, whose petals drooped over the vase.

The only life in the room was that of a cat,
Who scampered towards the door and past the disorienting smell
After several knocks and repeated name calls
Came from the other side of it.

That lonely cat whirled past the uniform pants who broke down the door,
And ran into the hallway —

# Marvin Gaye: What's Going on Trouble Man?

We wept for the world, on the brink of exploding.
We wept for our environment and Earth, poisoned.
We wept for Vietnam, senseless.
And we wept for the shining Prince of Motown —
We wept for our brother Marvin.

We wept that Tammi passed so young and cruelly.
We wept for Marvin Senior, who struck his son without mercy for
    any shortcoming.
We wept for Alberta, who watched her son fall by the hand of her husband.
We wept because, despite all the psychedelic gospel and soulful ballads,
No one came to Marvin, except the dark thoughts.

We wept for so long that it felt like a joke.
We wept that the Troubled Man was defenseless.
We wept because, despite his warnings for us, he himself had no protection,
And though he fashioned pure and raw peace in his voice,
He found none while on Earth.

We wept for the sensitive and handsome dark face in the limelight,
Smooth as the groove in a rainbow made of black seed and honey;
He offered his love for sale,
And we danced to his songs, but no one listened,
No one except the dark thoughts ....

## Before the Central Park Five Were Exonerated

When you look like this,
Things like justice and mercy are strained through a grater,
Resembling buckets and gallons of water sliced into lean droplets;
Fine pieces slip through the cracks,
But fail to leave real impact on black and brown surfaces.

Stripped of everything, except this skin, and what that entails,
I'm burning while slumped over in a gutter after all that's been thrown at me;
I plead not for freedom or wealth, or even standard living, but just water,
But still, you bash my skull with a gavel in one hand,
And a scepter of fire with the other…

# A Hip-Hop Promised Land

MCs rock back and forth
Like they were parishioners caught by the wisp of the Holy Ghost.

The cipher huddle,
With its rapid, improvised pace of rhymes and curse words, punchlines
    and slurs,
Sounds like the speaking of tongues to the uninitiated ear.

Human beatboxers
Chew throat kicks and throat clicks in their cheeks,
And their voices supplant the choir and organ as instruments.

The avenue block is littered
With the butts of cigarettes, which smell like expired ritual candles.

A hot dog cart parked at the curb,
Next to a storm drain that guzzles rainwater and stray-dog urine,
Becomes the place of fellowship after the makeshift posse cut.

And the summer playgrounds and bodega storefronts of Staten Island
Become beautiful, beautiful Zion —

# L.T. After Super Bowl XXI

Following the post-game speech, team prayer,
And journalist questions from various sporting publications,
Lawrence Taylor roped himself off
From the hoopla and revelry of the title-game celebration.

L.T. took a seat by himself on his stool by his locker booth,
Drenched in a settled sweat
And donning the remnants of confetti on his undershirt,
Scented with a yellow Gatorade bath.

He followed the violence all year long, as if it were a scrambler,
Taking all the quarterbacks, putting them in a burlap bag,
And then gleefully going upside it with a baseball bat.

But for over eight months starting tomorrow,
There was to be no more putting helmets square into the chests of quarterbacks,
Or causing left tackles in bed to stare at the ceiling long past midnight.

The off-season is a tightrope for Lawrence Taylor,
Regression and recovery.
Dispensing abuse, or succumbing to it.

The gladiator hero of our time cried to himself after winning the Super Bowl,
For the violence found within the sidelines was over,
And he knew the worst of it came when he was alone.

# How My Father Learned to Love the Mets

My father has rooted for the Mets only twice.
Most recently, and perhaps the final time in his life,
Was in the millennium's early Aughts,
When a brother, and one of his favorite Yankees,
Willie Randolph, was named manager,
And of course, the seasons leading up to and through the '86 season.

In the world of baseball,
Full of starched and Puritan Pat Boones,
The '86 Mets were great lightning rods of Little Richard cool.

The Yanks had long traded Reggie Jackson, the baddest ballplayer in the city,
And had yet to recover almost a decade later,
Despite the silver slugging and golden glove of Don Mattingly.

When the Bronx Zoo straightened up with their pinstripes
    and clean-cut hairdos,
The Mets were the sleazy, boys-will-be-boys bunch;
Hungover oddballs, who after picking the wedgies out of their pants,
Ran away with the pennant, a franchise-best 108 wins, and countless skirts.

It was the mid-'80s in New York, both in and out of Shea Stadium,
And there may as well have been a literal crack house in the dugout.
But for my father, and the city, and for a generation of men, it didn't matter.

If I was born, I also don't think I would've cared either
If Jesse Orosco or Doc Gooden
Were wiping the sweat from their eyes with a beer-soaked shirt while
    on the mound.

They were not the Miracles of '69, or had the grace to be Amazins',
But they were the toxic, Bad Guy ballplayers winning at the grand ol'game,
Beating everyone because of it, and that was cool, man.

# Jazzman Plays the Songbook

Tonight, the long cool is whittled down to the essentials of the essentials.
He is only one musician, and all the water and lip-licking in the world
Would not be enough for more than three hours of play.
Between *A Kiss to Build a Dream On* and *Darn that Dream,*
Bystanders pass to drop off coin in the porkpie
To honor his invocation of the ancient cries.
The past is brought back, and the old songs are wrung out
From atop his foldable stand, then sent out into the atmosphere;
The music pours into the street and rides the drift of the breeze,
Passing between pedestrians on Saturday night hikes seeking
metropolitan distractions.

# Idyllic Jazz Picnic

Summertime is the season
When hot lips not only scorch trumpets,
But can melt cones of ice cream.

Summer is the time of year
When mosquitoes are scratched and plucked,
And the sandlots are laced with players of swing.

The yardbirds live forever,
And soar the twilight sky
To see how high the Moon really is.

The dawn Sun is as golden brass as a horn,
And still can't blow the smoke
Or scale the heights of a saxophone.

The gods are still laughing at us, honey.

# Duke Ellington Leads the Cotton Club House Band

With the coaxing of a melody
From out his piano,
Duke cues Lady Ella to scat her notes,
Unspooling the music
From out her tonsils and soul.

With the curling of his
Ebony fingers on the ivory keys,
Duke unleashes the Satchmo: *Blow big man! Blow!*
Trumpet-tongued Louie sounds his song,
In every direction, all at once.

The music and culture
Lures white Harlem and Manhattan to the jungle,
Who long to see the roosters reign:
*But only a taste of the blackness —*

# The Last Dance at Paradise

Suppose that the music gathers dust in a forgotten warehouse somewhere,
Just sitting atop a stack of abandoned memories.
Suppose there was only the Cotton Club, welcoming black luminaries
   onto the stage,
But shutting the doors and putting away the tables for ordinary colored
   people.
Suppose there was no space for catharsis for Blacks in Upper Manhattan,
Living near-tragic and near-comic deriving from a particular city and
   consciousness.
Sure, the space to dance is not limited to just nightclubs,
But dames and dolls loved the communal environment,
Disarming menfolk with an eyelash or hip thrust, strutting with girlfriends,
And being in the presence of Mr. Bojangles himself;
Men wouldn't say much and would just follow the women wherever
   they went,
Harboring them in heavy coats on the sidewalk
And within their shoulders on the dancefloor.
But if there were no Prohibition cocktails to slug and swing down
   at that particular club,
And women weren't tossing their bashful shoes all around the dancehall,
It certainly would not sound like paradise to me.

## On Countee Cullen

If you were to throw yourself down
From the endless summit of the racial mountain,
Boundless and cruel as a nightmare,
Hoping they'd catch you at the bottom,
As if you were given charge of the angels....
After scaling these heights, and the line of Blake and Keats,
You'd figure that by melding your own dark voice in the sonnets,
Bidding that black and brown boys could indeed sing,
That the life net,
And water fountain, and dugouts, and bus seat, would be held open
For the colored artist who followed in the white footsteps and models,
But as you careened down to the ground, dreadfully fast, sinking down the sky,
You'd see that would not be the case.

# A Long Way from Jamaica

He wrote to clear his thoughts —
In 1919, they hung and put a match to a black man in Omaha.
A mob of 5,000, carrying ropes, baseball bats, and magnum shells
Sieged the courthouse, grabbed and strung William Brown to a
    telephone post,
And then tied his charred remains to a Packard,
Dragging his corpse throughout the avenues.
Claude McKay thought America would be beyond this archaic practice:
    mob rule,
And mistreating the innocent and desecrating the dead, like Achilles
    unto Hector,
But it wasn't…
Not even at the dawn of the millennium, with the murder of James Byrd jr.
So after observing such a bleak and bloody summer, the poet composes
    an anthem
That the Negro too, can and shall be prepared, to throw thunderbolts.

## To the Cab Driver Who Passed Me

Continue on your way, averting your eyes,
As if I were just another wandering squeegee man,
As they uncomfortably share a life story through a rolled-up window,
While shouting to remove the smudges from the windshield.

You pass by, without skipping a beat, though I see an empty backseat.
I will not cry aloud, and I will even put down my arm, and wait for
   the next one.

What remains, in your car, and your utter being,
As I fade out of your rearview and your existence, like a distant memory,
Is an ugliness more hostile and dangerous than all the things
You actually think I would do to you; as if your being warrants such
attention from me.

## Flight from the City

They surrendered the city.
Black and brown teenagers were popping up, huddling on street corners
Where they used to walk their sweater-wearing pups and get coffee.
In the subways, and on the bus,
They would hear languages in different-sounding tongues,
So they fled, like deli napkins in a spanking gust,
Or like patriot garrisons after the British captured Long Island.
When the colors became too much,
They journeyed past the darkness,
Past the ebony and yellow and brown hands who worked this ivory world,
Trying to get a piece of their own.
So they left the city, holing up in suburbs and villages up the Hudson.

# A Puerto Rican Dance Festival

Despite the pan-fried heat of late summer
Having long depleted the colors out of the green
On a festive San Juan street,
Brown people, lots of them,
Acrobatic, flirtatious, and melting into all sorts of possibilities,
Volley themselves as couples lift each other,
Flying in an air of carnival and musical vibration,
Soaking the sky with smiles beaded in sweat.
In the waning stage light of sundown,
Dancing bodies press in and sway, leaning on from fatigue,
And are ready to put to bed, muscles, as well the eyes of lovers.

# Thanksgiving: Balloon Handler Blues

An early Nor'easter ricochets up the Eastern Seaboard;
The winds of the cold front snap, and the ropes are tangled,
And despite all force and instructions from parade monitors,
Despite all pulling and tugging,
Underdog and Felix the Cat find themselves in an unintentional tussle,
As aerial neighborhoods and high rises have ringside seats
To balloon floats holding on to each other,
Like weary heavyweights, deep in the final rounds.
All the while, bundled-up paradegoers and balloon handlers
Are pummeled and pelted by the frigid gusts of late November.

## On Wise Whitman

Leave me nothing
But the common folk,
And their litanies in response to the world.

For their conduct of life,
Let me see their tear-run, smiling faces,
And touch their crippling hunger of bread, and ambition.

Flow their unknowing, realized passions
In my veins, and let my words bleed
And breathe in the deep understanding
That creation is alive, and throbbing —

## On the Prologue of Melville and the Epilogue of Ellison

The ocean's slumber is interrupted
By neck-sliced body snatchers, being flung into its waters.
Slaves overtaking their capturers in the dead of night,
Witnessed only by a mounted, yellow moon in the sky,
Dance in reveille under the light.

Elsewhere out of time....

The unnamed narrator
Taps the light bulbs above his head;
Little, yellow globes soak their shine into the cellar walls.
Having escaped the world, he lets out a breath and dances,
And his celebratory skin is a jumping shadow off the incandescents.

# Jamaicans in the Orchard

At the end of the day, the Jamaicans return from the pasture,
Hauling buckets and drums of apples,
As darkness borders the edge of the sun.
These isle-bred, farmhand sugarcane cutters
Are a long way from the tropics,
Being so far north and being so close to the St. Lawrence.
The walk is far from the orchard to the trucks,
As the closer they approach the vehicles,
The more the fields and trees dissolve out of detail from the distance.
For the workday, they pick and snap apples off branches
And divide the smooth fruits against the ones with bruises;
They go back to their temporary lodging after such peculiar labor,
And dine on jerk chicken, for it's Jerk Chicken Wednesdays.
And so is the harvest ritual, until winter, when they return to Jamaica.

# Scenic Sunday Drive Upstate

Suppose that the road upstate,
Flanked by orchards and dotted by bed-and-breakfast lodges,
Were actually endless, and did not merely feel endless
Due to the presence and frequent, speed-bump interruptions
Of colonial-size villages and hamlets requiring 30 MPH speed limits.
If there were no need to decelerate our engine,
And autumn drives on mountainous Sundays were truly without
    restrictions,
I would loop back again, continuously,
And repeatedly drive past the orchards and bed-and-breakfast lodges.
I would drive northward always,
At a tempo meant for the hurried world of the city, until the car
    became unsalvageable,
And I would be pleasantly stuck in those same villages and hamlets,
Encircled by the mountains, whose luster when the sun hits,
Is simply perfect.

# Buzzards Descend from the Clouds

Vultures, stalking in the pasture of vast, rolling clouds,
Thrust their beaks through the Cumulus
After catching wind and being charmed by the smell lying on the Earth,
Battered and splitter-splattered on the roadway.

Parasites and a nest of crows, amassed around the thick-coated hide,
Scatter upon being caught
In the shadowed wing of nature's pecking order,
Descending out of the clouds to partake in death, like devils disguised
as angels.

# Friday Night in a College Town

As buskers and local a cappella groups
Jam, blow, strum, and sob their songs outside of taverns,
A music too real to be renowned,
The coeds drink and converse
Of their experiences in the bars and night cafés,
While fraternity members,
Swarming onto the avenue, like hornets out the nest,
Drift and pub crawl to another tab,
As wingmen gas up brothers in front of potential lovers —

## Outdoor Black Cat Blues

Outdoor black cats are not as fortunate as people.
When human drunks are told to leave bars or nightclubs,
With vacant, alcoholic eyes,
They thumb through their phones for rideshare apps to take them home,
Or with thumbs of foolery, hail down a passing, yellow car.

Outdoor black cats, wandering in and out of neighborhoods,
When ordered to leave the backyard stoop
By screaming mouths or the bristle head of a broom,
Return to the alleyways under terrible silence,
And stretch out on their backs, to swipe at passing stars.

## An Innocent Black Bear Sighting

There was not any property damage, or bluffs of charging anyone.
The fences on the street stayed upright through the night,
And the garbage bins remained undisturbed with trash sealed
   under their lids.
There was no roar that peeled back the peace of a hushed village;
There were just farmers, putting away their garden tools,
Nimbly tiptoeing inside their barns and behind silos
After catching sight of an unexpected, black fur passing through,
And a college town clique, returning from a night on the town,
In their distorted vision, believing they were merely chucking beer bottles
At an oddly shaped waste bin.

# On Visiting Cooperstown

Mere outfielders and relief pitchers are given rank and footing
Akin to Roman emperors, or U.S. presidents, in the great corridor,
Lined with the sculpted busts of ballplayers.
Great Sultans of Swat, with hands like hams,
Best suited for destroying ballparks, seemingly extend theirs to
    shake mine.

As I wander through the names and faces that have marked
    the time across two centuries,
The bronze of Cap Anson shoots daggers for my mere presence
    in this hallowed place,

But it is the busts of colored ballplayers, who I drink in like
    summertime lemonade,
Or captivating literature, that makes me feel welcome.

The physical anger and subliminal sadness of racism are enough
    for my soul to spasm,

And when I arrive at the stern visage of Rube Foster, the
    commissioner of black baseball,
My heart is broken for how his life and spirit fell under from such
    hatred.

## Pedro Strikes Out 17 at Yanks


Though they were hated Boston, and we were New York,
As the bottom-half frames played out much the same, a mastery on
   the art of pitching,
Hearing the Dominicans in the back rows of Section 39,
Gradually growing in confidence
As they belted out his name with accented lungs with each K:
*Pedro! Pedro! Pedro!*
And zealously unfurled and waved their flags in celebration
As if they themselves had won the war....
Was bigger than baseball.

## Binghamton June

In summer,
The wide, brushstroke daylight of the Allegheny Plateau
Never bothers the farm girls tending their gardens,
Or the mountain men, hiking the hills
And streams of the Susquehanna.

In summer,
The clouds coiling 'round the mounds,
Suffocate the sun, and spill autumn,
For in that low-hanging, morning June fog,
There's plenty of 50-degree days to be found.

# Lunchtime at Lupo's S&S Char Pit

You can always tell when it's the lunchtime rush.
There are clouds of black, charred smoke spewing out,
Frying up pork and chicken skewers, and crinkly fries on the grill.
Scented smoke floats to the roof of the shack's ceiling,
Trickling out of the chimney, then straight above,
Populating the grey, overcast sky of the rolling hills with darkness;
They're cooking up so many orders, and there's so much black
   cloud cover,
It looks as if heaven itself were burning.

# The Death Certificate of Gil Scott-Heron

It was death by New York,
While trying to save Detroit...

# After the Audubon Ballroom, Feb. 1965

The girls were scared, and a pregnant Betty tried to console
  and squash
The fear like their father had done, like an avenging angel,
Across a nation of households, and not just their own.

Those in the back of the overflow
At the Unity Funeral Home squint their eyes
To watch the Beloved peer down on him,
Wrapped and laid in ivory robes of ceremony.

Ruby Dee and Ossie Davis, strained from emotion,
Recite telegrams and cables of condolences from home and abroad
  into microphones.
Davis consecrates the brother in eulogy with a swelling voice,
Akin to the adoration of the children of Israel when David slew the
  Philistines.

The widowed wife and young children go home;
Funds are to be raised to care for the girls,
And a new home, perhaps in Westchester or Putnam.

The inaudible gunfire and wailing
That terrorizes in nightmares,
Repeats and repeats, like a sorrowful, haunting lullaby.

The empty spirit in the house becomes a reminder of terrible news.

The world lost a prophet,
And Betty Shabazz asks for privacy to lament in solitude
Her husband, and the father to her children...

# An Opinion Piece on the Death of Newsprint

I miss holding newspapers
Like I miss seeing forecasts of snow,
And stories about the deaths of dictators.
I miss the versatility of newsprint,
Such as scrunching day-old comics into balls,
To soak up my poured-on soles.
I miss the Sunday football predictions, which made the pundits
Look like Monday fools.
There was still more for the world to do
In the age of newsprint:
Like using two-day columns as barbeque cleaner, and gift wrap.
I liked catching and highlighting typos like other kids caught fireflies
    in summer.
I often wondered who would contact the elderly Sterling household
For the litter of puppies they were trying to sell?
I even miss reading the stories which sank my heart,
Since that's when I knew journalists were needed, and were working.

## Expats in the Gershwin's "Mademoiselle in New Rochelle"

Still over there, the Americans were in Paris,
Long after reason, for Yankee soldiers had already toppled the Huns.
But, by the Seine River,
They angle and cast their nets for mermaids,
Trusting that a good haul
Would mean never having to return to New York.

# Jersey Boardwalk Vacation

There weren't jet skis racing on the water, and the boardwalk throng,
Usually clustered with beachgoers and city slickers
Trying to cram in the final crumbs of summer,
Was hauntingly sparse for the Labor Day weekend.
Bathing suits have been traded in for jackets and windbreakers on
    the beach.
Children tease the shore, running to its edge,
But then retreat with blissful screams as the great waves lap upon
    the shore,
Then return to the ocean.
There is no sun in Wildwood this weekend,
And picture-perfect postcards will have to be photographed another day.

This photograph was taken some time in the late 1980s, in East Rutherford, New Jersey, outside of the old Giants' Stadium. The man pictured on the right is my father, Michael, and to the left, is his older brother, Jeffrey. While Michael saw many professional games around this time at Giants Stadium, including the historic Flipper Anderson Game in 1989, this tailgate was for the black college football game, the Whitney M. Young Jr. Memorial Football Classic.

This photograph was taken in the summer of 1993 in the Bronx neighborhood of City Island. The woman pictured is my mother, Wynne, and she is holding my older brother, Aaron. For those unfamiliar with the state of New York, New Rochelle and its county, Westchester, are a suburb to the Bronx and New York City.

# ACKNOWLEDGMENTS

Grateful acknowledgment is made to the journals in which the following poems appeared, sometimes as different versions:

*Chronogram Magazine:* "A Prescription from Dr. J"
*Corvus Review:* "On Wise Whitman"
*The Front Porch Review:* "Puerto Rican Dance Festival"
*Ghost City Review:* "An Opinion Piece on the Death of Newsprint"
*The Hudson Valley Writer's Guild:* "Friday Night in a College Town,"
   "Scenic Sunday Drive Upstate," and "On Visiting Cooperstown"
*Maudlin House:* "Dark Comedy"
*The Museum of Americana:* "The Last Dance at Paradise"
*The Occulum:* "Big Apple Blues"
*Plum Tree Tavern:* "Binghamton June"
*The Roanoke Review:* "Dark Comedy"
*The South Florida Poetry Journal:* "Gin-Soaked Saxophone Solo"

# NOTES

In several poems in this collection, pieces of art, film, literature, and music are referenced and/or were inspirations. For verses that do not directly express or state these allusions, below are a list of references featured and the corresponding poem they are in:

"On Washington Irving and his Literary Friends at Sunnyside": 1864 painting of the same title by Charles Schussler and Felix Octavius.

"The Last Dance at Paradise": Small's Paradise, a popular nightclub in New York City during the Harlem Renaissance.

"On Countee Cullen": Harlem Renaissance poet, Countee Cullen, who was greatly inspired by the British Romantics, and Langston Hughes' 1926 essay, "The Negro Arist and the Racial Mountain."

"A Long Way from Jamaica": Jamaican immigrant and Harlem Renaissance Writer, Claude McKay, whose most recognizable poem, "If We Must Die," was published amid the racial violence of 1919's Red Summer.

"On the Prologue of Melville and the Epilogue of Ellison:" The short story, "Benito Cereno," by Herman Melville and the novel, *Invisible Man,* by Ralph Ellison.

"Jamaicans in the Orchards": The 2017 New York Times' article: "The Jamaican Apple Pickers of Upstate New York."

"Cause of Death Certificate: Gil Scott-Heron": The songs, "New York is Killing Me" and "We Almost Lost Detroit" by Gil Scott-Heron.

"Expats in the Gershwin's Mademoiselle in New Rochelle": The 1927 musical by Ira and George Gershwin, *Strike Up the Band."*

# THANK YOU

I would first like to thank God, whose grace has made me succeed in all my pursuits.

My parents, Michael and Wynne, to whom I am forever indebted for the lessons and stories they have shared. Your care and encouragement are the foundation of not just this collection, but who I am as a person, and I hope these poems stand as a testament to what you've taught me. My siblings, Jessica, Aaron, and Daniel, whom I adore and who continue to inspire me with their work, encouragement, and love. My extended family members on both the Johnson and Brewington side; I know I should call more often, but I absolutely love you all, and your support is invaluable and truly an inspirational force.

Justin Vernold, thank you again my friend for providing honest and encouraging feedback on this collection; my writing was elevated thanks to your expertise. Thank you, Aaron Dylan Graham, Grant Clauser, and Rochelle Spencer, for taking the time to review this collection and provide your honest and kind opinions. I must continue to praise the work of the teachers I've studied under, from Sensational Shiloh Baptist Church in New Rochelle to Zion Lutheran and St. Augustine in Bridgeport, CT, and the English Department at UNC-Greensboro (with special consideration for Professor Noelle Morrissette); thank you for exposing me to many of the ideas found in this collection. I must also thank Larry Moffi, whose mentorship and advice continues to help me grow as a writer, and with whom I've deeply enjoyed having conversations.

This collection would not be possible without the support and service of Raymond Hammond and the staff at The New York Quarterly Foundation. Your special interest and dedication in helping me with this project is deeply appreciated, and I am sincerely grateful for the finished product. Thank you for your tireless work to make this collection a reality, as it has truly been a pleasure.